STEAM MEMORIES: 1940's-1960's

PETE WATERMAN'S

SWINDON

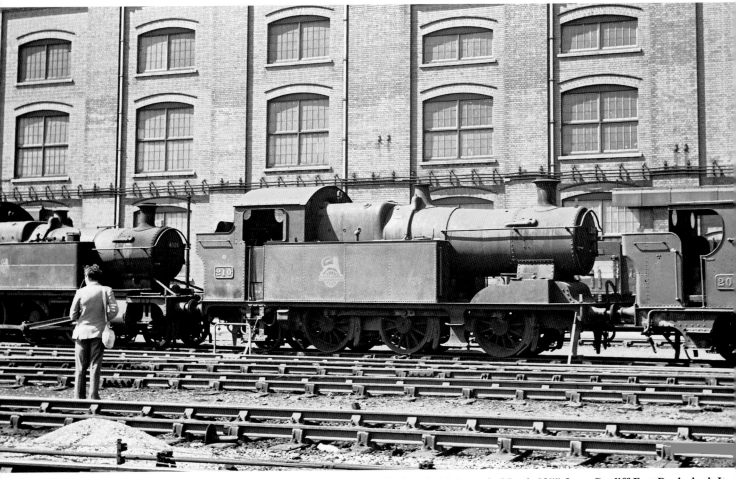

Diversity at Swindon. No.210 was a former Taff Vale engine built in 1907 and withdrawn in March 1955 from Cardiff East Dock shed. It is seen here in the works on 24th June 1955.

(*previous page*) **August 1957 – 'Dukedog' No.9025 had just been withdrawn from Oswestry shed. It is indeed a blessing that today we can still see one of these classic looking engines.**

Printed and bound by The Amadeus Press, Cleckheaton, West Yorkshire
First published in the United Kingdom by Book Law Publications, 382 Carlton Hill, Nottingham, NG4 1JA

PETE & TOMMY'S ADVENTURE AT SWINDON

Now there can be fewer things in life that have made me laugh so much as the day that Tommy turned up in his short trousers. Tommy, not famous for his sartorial elegance, found it difficult to look 'normal' in long trousers but in short trousers he stood no chance. Being a bit on the 'tubby' side he looked altogether wrong and for some reason he reminded me of a Christmas pudding!

"OK Tom! I give up! What's the joke?" Knowing Tommy as only I did, I knew there would be a long, drawn out explanation and I braced myself to hear it! I didn't have long to wait since without a nod or even a hint of disapproval at my laughter, he replied, very earnestly, "Well Pete, I thought we could bunk off school next Wednesday and go to Swindon so we could do the afternoon guided tour".

As always, I wasn't sure whether Tommy was being serious - his expression gave nothing away and since I was referring to him wearing short trousers anyway, I was a bit thrown by this reply so I asked Tom to explain the relevance of the short trousers and the corresponding woolly socks! "Ah", he said, "It's obvious isn't it – we've got to be able to fool the station ticket office that we are under 12 years old so that we can get to Swindon for half fare so I thought I'd test the con out on you!" Like he said, it was obvious - well to Tommy it was!

Whilst you can applaud the fact that Tom had obviously thought this through and planned for all eventualities, there was no way on earth that we were going to fool anybody into thinking that we were eligible for half fare and, with the greatest respect to Tommy's forward planning, the short trousers were never going to be the clincher! In fact, if I'm being truthful, when I weighed everything up I decided that I'd rather pay full fare and sit in another carriage, than travel looking that stupid with a companion looking more stupid. So I pointed this out to Tommy who replied that he didn't have enough pocket money left for the fare if we had to pay full price - which was a fair point - so we agreed to see if we could fine tune the wardrobe a bit!

Then a far greater concern occurred to me and I said to Tommy "Hey, Tom are we not running away with ourselves here because what do we tell our Mums who sets their clocks by us getting back at 4.05pm every day from Freddy's?"

 "We'll tell them we're playing rugby." Tommy replied "Away from home" he added just to add a bit of weight to the explanation!

"But Tom, they know that we don't play a school in Swindon" I astutely pointed out.

"Well don't mention Swindon," he replied (not unreasonably). However, we both agreed that even if we had said that we were playing Copthorne, which was the furthest school from Freddy's, then we would still have to have dawdled an awful lot to get home as late as 9pm so we thought it better to say that we were going to a mate's house to watch telly.

Wednesday couldn't come soon enough and off we went with our egg sandwiches, duffel bags and yes, you've guessed it, we were both in short trousers! Well it must have been our lucky day or, as is said today, 'he should have gone to Specsavers', because believe it or not we did purchase two half-price fares to Swindon via Leamington Spa. A phrase my Mum used to say to me to put me back in my place was - "You're not as big as you think you are!" and this was obviously true way back then when Tommy and I thought we looked far too 'old' for half fare.

All the way there we were getting very excited about the fact that we were going to have a full half day walking around what we both believed to be the best railway works in the world – Swindon - and we'd be legitimate (well almost, if you forgot we were bunking off school) since all we had to do after lunch was to join a queue and for half a crown we would be shown around the whole works. Believe me that was so much better than being slung out on your ear which had happened to me on so many occasions after I'd snuck in somewhere!

It was only a short walk from Swindon station to the works and, full of enthusiasm, we approached the works gates where there was already a queue forming. To be honest we could hardly contain our excitement - I'd actually taken three pens just in case one ran out! What hit us first was the immense size of the place and for two urchins from Coventry this was bigger than our imaginations!

As we took in the enormity of this fantastic place, for some inexplicable reason, it was at this point, that Tommy remembered we should have been at school and worse still that we should have been having a lesson with Mr. (Taffy) Griffiths, our History teacher! Mr. Griffiths was one of those teachers who put the fear of death into us and who was nobody's fool. Since both Tommy and I were 'no shows', he would know that we were up to something together! I was ready to dismiss Tommy's point because in my mind the pleasure of being there, at that moment, outweighed the pain of the punishment we would both receive at the hands of the dreaded Mr. Griffiths, but reality hit me and I tried to get my head around what we should do about it when, out of the blue, our problem was solved by the most unlikely source!

A dirty great hand descended on my shoulder followed by the words "Waterman, you blessed goon what are you and Tommy doing here? You should both be at school!" I turned quickly, although I would have recognised that voice anywhere, and sure enough there was Taffy Griffiths looking at me with thunder in his eyes! My first thought was "well, I could say the same to you Sir" – but I thought better of it and said the only thing that anybody could say at that point – "I didn't know you were a train spotter Sir!" I could see Tommy out of the corner of my eye and he looked ashen but he said nothing. Gradually the expression on Mr. Griffiths' changed from one of superiority to one of almost guilt as he was absolutely dumbstruck when he realised that although he'd caught me and Tommy in short trousers, he'd been caught with his trousers down! He said absolutely nothing, took his hand off my shoulder and with a funny kind of nod, he very quickly disappeared into the crowd.

"No need to worry about facing Mr. Griffiths tomorrow eh Tom? We can relax and enjoy our day at Swindon Works."

We had a fantastic day - not even our Mums asked any awkward questions and we both actually looked forward to our next history lesson because we knew that when Mr. Griffiths started to talk about 'Kings' Tommy and I would find it very difficult not to laugh!

Pete Waterman, South Bank, October 2011.

The contents of this album illustrate many of the locomotive types which have graced the rails of that erstwhile but nevertheless great locomotive works. It would have been nice to have seen all of the engines illustrated during the visit described above but alas that was not the case. However, Swindon never did disappoint its visitors and my one afternoon 'bunking' off school was followed by many more visits to Swindon which were just as enjoyable. Hopefully, this album conveys the excitement and thrill experienced during my numerous visits to the home of the former Great Western Railway.

Unless otherwise credited, the majority of the illustrations within this album came from the Neville Stead collection.

It has long been accepted by railway enthusiasts that the identity of a steam locomotive at the end of its working life was not necessarily the exact same locomotive which was put into traffic at the start of its life. The usual suspects which were changed during a locomotive's lifetime were the boilers and, if a tender engine, a swap of tender perhaps. Other parts were changed for new as they wore out whereas some parts were refurbished and used on other engines of the same class. 'Castle' class No.7027 THORNBURY CASTLE was typical in having some of the above mentioned changes but it also underwent other changes too, as described below. Built in August 1949, and withdrawn in December 1963, it is seen in this 1957 photograph with a Standard 4000 gallon Collett tender – it went into traffic with a Hawksworth flat-sided tender. Until April 1960 it was an Old Oak Common engine but during that month it transferred to Worcester and so became one of the last operational examples of the class. BR sold it too Woodham Brothers at Barry after which it was purchased by Birmingham Railway Museum and subsequently sold on to the Waterman Railway Heritage Trust. Sister 'Castle' No.5029 NUNNEY CASTLE, which also ended up at Barry when BR discarded it, was involved in a mishap either at Barry or whilst en route to that place. When No.5029 was eventually purchased from Woodham's, prior to No.7027's sale, the good bogie from 7027 was swapped for the damaged bogie on 5029! However, there is more to reveal. When No.7027 was secured by the Waterman RHT, it was found that the inside motion is in fact from two different 'Star' class engines. The axle boxes came from either large 'Prairies' or 'Kings' – in fact the only 7027 numbers found stamped on the engine are on the frames!

Gloucester based 'Star' No.4059 LADY PATRICIA stands at Swindon works in mid-1952, just before withdrawal. The engine appears to have just arrived on works as it is not in steam but coal still fills the tender. As it has yet to be stripped of its coal, the 4-6-0 may not yet have been condemned. Therefore, the date could well be late August or early September. What is certain is the livery which is wartime GWR without the crest although the beading was removed a long time before the Second World War. The circular plate on the side of the smokebox shows this Standard No.1 boiler once had outside steam pipes ('Castle' type outside steam pipes were fitted to this engine in August 1944), a new smokebox at this late stage in its life would have been out of the question. Built in July 1914, this particular lady has a short safety valve and the typical tall thin chimney.

Churchward 'Saint' No.2934 BUTLEIGH COURT on shed at Swindon in June 1950. Just short of being forty years old, this 4-6-0 was in BR black lined livery with the small emblem adorning its 3,500 gallon tender (note the larger version on the Prairie tank to the right). Both number and name plates have a red background. Built in November 1911, No.2934 was fitted with outside steam pipes in November 1938. Note that the valve spindle covers on the front end resemble square boxes. With a cast-iron shed plate yet to be fitted, the engine's home depot is identified by the SDN painted on the vertical surface of the running plate above the cylinder. Fairly recent additions include the speedo' on the back wheel nut and the GWR version of AWS. Withdrawn in June 1952, No.2934 was broken up a month later.

The former Landore based locomotive which is the subject of this 13th February 1955 photograph was withdrawn some three years and seven months earlier, in July 1951! Wearing GWR wartime livery, the rods, number and name plates are all missing for a very good reason – this is No.4003 LODE STAR, the one chosen to go to the railway museum. Built in February 1907, the engine was fitted with a No.3 superheater in 1911, whilst the elbow-type steam pipes were acquired as late as March 1949. However, what is really interesting about this illustration is that the livery looks too good for an engine that had been out of traffic for such a long time.

8

After a lifetime at Stourbridge, 'Prairie' No.5147 spent the final four months of its operational life in Cornwall. The 'Large Prairies' were fairly rare in the south-west so the 2-6-2Ts transfer to Truro in October 1952 would have been a welcome change however, the trend was to continue as No.5147 was withdrawn during the following January. Built as No.3147 in March 1906, this engine was part of the first batch of Large Prairies. Rebuilt in 1927 with a Standard No.2 boiler, the 2-6-2T was renumbered into the 51XX series. Two things tell us that it was a rebuild – the square drop front and the bunker rivet pattern. Note also that the boiler has a smokebox patch for outside steam pipes. Scrutiny of the illustration, which was captured at Swindon on 10th May 1953, suggests that No.5147 had been out of use for longer than twelve weeks indicated by the dates. Paint has gone from the smokebox in patches and you can actually see it lifting!

This ex-Cardiff Railway 0-6-2T was withdrawn from Cardiff East Dock shed in September 1953 and was photographed at Swindon on 22nd November waiting to be broken up. As an independent concern, the Cardiff Railway had thirty-six locomotives but two had been cut up by the time it was absorbed by the GWR. Built in 1908 by Kitsons, as CR No.35, No.155 was rebuilt in 1928 with a coned boiler by the GW at Caerphilly – the only Cardiff engine to carry the Standard No.3 boiler (GWR Diagram A41). Classified 4F by British Railways, the smokebox numberplate was added in 1949. Note the blackout side sheets on the cab.

Going back to 16th February 1950 now and we find ex-Whitland & Cardigan Railway 0-6-0ST No.1331 on the dump waiting for the inevitable. Another 'old-timer' it had certainly been around having served at Weymouth, Swindon and Oswestry amongst other depots. Re-conditioned at Wolverhampton in 1946, this was the last of all the absorbed engines from the years 1854-1921.

'2021' Class No.2148 was withdrawn from Laira in February 1952. Initially built as saddle tanks, the class was a product of the Wolverhampton factory, and were turned out from 1897 to 1905; No.2148 was built in July 1904. Rebuilt with pannier tanks from January 1923, these 0-6-0s were small but very pretty engines (and a great favourite of mine) of which 110 of the original 140 were still in traffic at Nationalisation. The last to be converted from a saddletank was No.2048 in 1948; it too succumbed to scrap in 1952. Considerable inroads had been made into the class by the scrapman during the first four years of BR and by 1958 the '2021' class was down to one member – No.2069 - working from Birkenhead, it was withdrawn in April 1959. In this 10th May 1953 photograph No.2148 appears to be part of the Swindon works shunting fleet, the 3-link and screw couplings being part and parcel of such work at Swindon, however, it was cut up during the following August. Note the buffer beam sitting above the footplate so that the buffers were raised to wagon height. I have an apprentice-made model of the working valve gear of one of those made in Wolverhampton in the early 1900s which is still painted with Indian red frames, double lining and a saddletank! I was lucky enough to see one of the last examples still working since, as a carriage warmer, No.2067 was
at Leamington until late 1959 - well past its withdrawal date of November 1952!

No.258 was a Barry Railway 0-6-2T (their No.76) built in December 1894 by Sharp Stewart and withdrawn by British Railways in November 1949. Seen here circa late-1952, the six-coupled tank has followed the route of many former pre-Group engines from South Wales in finding employment at Swindon long after withdrawal. No.258 managed to stay active until May 1953 which indicates that it must have been in good condition when initially condemned as the last one in service in 1949. Although some of the class received smokebox number plates, No.258 did not; it also still had GWR on the side tanks. Note the injector pipes – they are fairly basic – also the holes in the frames.

No.1925 was another product of Wolverhampton and was put into traffic in December 1883 as a member of '850' Class. Many were converted to Panniers but No.1925, along with sixteen others, managed to take its saddletanks to the scrapyard. Equipped with H-spoke wheels (like LNWR wheels) these engines too had a deep bufferbeam which was raised to line-up the buffers to the standard wagon height. Being small, and having a short wheelbase, this class was useful in yards with tight curvature track work. Withdrawn in April 1951, No.1925 did not have far to travel to Swindon scrapyard; a Southall shed code (SHL) shows on the valance whilst the smokebox door carries a cast shed plate showing 81D Reading! Also in the picture on this rather wet but undated occasion is a 'Star' with elbow steam pipes (No.4058 PRINCESS AUGUSTA was withdrawn April 1951 and had the elbow steam pipes). A tenderless, and unidentified 'Bulldog' of the 'Bird' series resides behind the 0-6-0ST.

Back to (or is that forward to) 10th May 1953. Filling the frame now is Pannier No.1287, a former member of the '1076' or 'Buffalo' Class, which was withdrawn in April 1946, some seven years previously. Built in January 1878 at Swindon as a saddletank, No.1287 was converted to a Pannier in February 1925. Withdrawn in June 1939, the six-coupled tank was re-instated to traffic on the outbreak of WWII. The next withdrawal came well after the ending of hostilities but stretching its luck even further, No.1287 went on to Stationary Boiler duties, firstly at Newbury, then at Leamington Spa. It carried five different boilers during its lifetime but the last one finally pegged-out in early 1953 and by October No.1287 was cut up. On the left is small Prairie No.4512 which had been condemned in February 1953 – note the chalked 'Cond' below the number plate – no doubt requiring new frames. During the previous decade many of the 45XX class were due new frames but after the War they were withdrawn unless their frames were in good condition. For their part BR replaced the 45XXs with the small BR Standards. All accountants, please sit on your hands.

No.2195 was a former Burry Port & Gwendraeth Valley Railway 0-6-0ST built by Avonside in April 1905 as BP&GVR No.5. It was first withdrawn in March 1939 but was then re-instated in December of that year to help the war effort. At that time its original name CWN MAWR, which it had carried to March 1939, was not refitted (perhaps that had gone into the melting pot to make a shell case or two). It was finally withdrawn in January 1953 and in this 14th June 1953 photograph it appears to have been recently active, no doubt as a works shunter. It was finally scrapped during the following November. Note the holes in the tank where the nameplate was once displayed; also, the position of the 82C shedplate is unusual but not unique amongst the smaller locomotives employed by BR. Classmate No.2194 was condemned and scrapped in February 1953.

BP&GVR No.7 PEMBREY was built at Avonside Engine Co., in Bristol in 1907. It lost its name during an overhaul at Swindon between 1923 and 1927. Withdrawal took place in March 1955. Although smaller than No.2195, another ex-BP&GVR Avonside-built locomotive featured in this album, No.2176 has a crosshead-driven vacuum pump whereas No.2195 did not, although they were both classified 1F under BR. If your study the photograph of No.2195, you will see it still had its original tanks. No.2176, shown here on 21st June 1955, has a shorter bunker and interestingly has not carried black-out shutters. It had 3ft 9in. wheels and you will note that the cab handrails are in different positions whilst the cylinders were the same on both engines – although clad in different ways.

We see so many photographs taken at this spot – but why not! Centre of attention in this 12th August 1956 exposure is 'County' class No.1026 COUNTY OF SALOP which is fresh out of shops in its new green livery. At that time she was a Shrewsbury engine, as indeed she was for most of her life. New in January 1947, it went from Swindon to Old Oak Common the same week that I was born. As a youngster, I saw this engine every week and it was one of those which you assumed would always be around when 'spotting'; I do remember thinking that No.1026 always appeared as though it was cherished. You can see that it was a hot day when this photograph was taken, because all the windows in the shed are open to get some air through the place – with a glass roof, ventilation would have been essential to all those working on the shop floor!

After withdrawal during the previous month, this is No.2409 at Swindon on 10th May 1953. Built here in November 1891, this is the classic Dean Goods which became one of the largest classes on the Great Western. They were everywhere and they were even sent overseas in both world wars. A handful made it into BR power class 2MT in black livery, with No.2579 being lined out in LNWR black – it looked crackin! The tender in this illustration is as old as the engine, being one of the Dean 3500 gallon examples. The locomotive is fitted with ATC and it was withdrawn from Brecon shed but had been at Oswestry for sometime. I never saw one in steam but I did see one at Swindon before it went into the museum and it was spectacular.

6000 KING GEORGE V – 25th April 1954. You could write a book just about this locomotive. The photograph says it all though. Built in June 1927, it went to Bristol but from 1952 it was an Old Oak engine. This engine could be seen every two days on the 'Wolverhampton's'. I was there again at Leamington to witness it brake the steam ban with the Bulmers train and every year I just wanted to spend five minutes on the footplate. I think back to the 1950s when I would stand at Leamington and see the bell come round the corner. This 'King' was not one of those painted blue as that honour went to Nos.6001, 6009, 6025 and 6026.

'Pannier' No.8758 on 22nd August 1954. Built at Swindon in November 1933, and withdrawn in January 1959 from Southall. This is the later type of 57XX with a rounded top cab which could be lifted off to allow access to the inner cab – you can see the row of rivets. This engine has welded tanks and, of course, this was the Standard shunter on the Western and could be seen everywhere. Although there was only on Class 57XX, there were lots of differences within the 'Pannier' classes built subsequently. The cabs, as I've already mentioned, were riveted and the top feed was moved around or was not fitted at all. A 57XX 0-6-0PT was the first engine I fired and I have had a lot of fun on them over the years. Coincidentally, it was a 57XX boiler that was our first big job at our works in Crewe.

'Modified Hall' No.7918 ROSE WOOD HALL on 13th February 1955. This is how I remember Rosewood – black with the big lion and another Leamington regular. Built in April 1950, it was always a Tyseley engine until withdrawn in February 1965. The engine was a Hawksworth modification and the lubricator was fitted sideways so they could work from a small rocker arm. When I look at this photograph I'm prompted to ask, "Is there any wonder why I love the Western Region, and why did I spend so much of my time there?" Yes, I know they are supposed to be Brunswick green but I love that LNWR livery. The Oxford 'Halls' were the black 'Halls' which had red backing to their names and numbers.

Visiting Swindon on 6th May 1956, ex-Cardiff Railway No.1338 was based at Taunton throughout the 1950s, going to Swansea East Dock in June 1960. When I was young my family spent most of our summer holidays at Minehead, Blue Anchor Bay or Dunster, and I always made my Dad stop at Taunton to see this particular locomotive, although he would never let me take a photograph of it since we always needed to keep the film for the holidays! Built as Cardiff Railway No.5 in 1898, this engine is now preserved and can be seen at Didcot. Note that the valve gear and motion are very unusual in this photograph where the safety valve springs can be seen.

On 9th April 1961 Reading based 'Hall' No.6953 LEIGHTON HALL was coming to the end of a major overhaul, probably its last, and is about to have a fire put in prior to running-in. Built in February 1943, it ran un-named until April 1947. A month later it was converted to burn oil and renumbered 3953. It reverted back to coal firing in September 1948 as the Coal Crisis eased. Very good looking mixed traffic locomotives, the 'halls' were amongst the last ex-GWR engines running as steam traction gave way to diesel. An Old Oak stalwart from 1950 to 1959, it ended up at Oxford where it was withdrawn in December 1965.

This is 'Castle' No.7013 BRISTOL CASTLE on 12th November 1956. Built in June 1948 – well not quite – the engine featured is actually No.4082 WINDSOR CASTLE, built in 1924! Re-numbered in February 1952, it was a Worcester engine then and later allocated to Old Oak. It ended its days at Tyseley in September 1964. I loved the 'Castles' which, in their Brunswick green with the big lion, looked great. This was another locomotive I saw a lot of, and it was easy to spot as the front cover was of the earlier type – the class had three types of front covers.

'Britannia' No.70028 ROYALSTAR was built at Crewe in December 1952 and was allocated to Canton for most of its life. This photograph of 22nd March 1953 is interesting as it shows the old style handrail on the smoke deflectors. The Pacific looks to be out of steam although it had been working since there is water coming from the injectors and the patina on the boiler cladding shows signs of heat and oil. However, the windows are spotless. Note the oil storage boxes in the foreground. I had to include this photograph because 'Brits' at Swindon were not that common a sight.

13th February 1955 – Its that favoured position again but this time we have 'Castle' No.7011 BANBURY CASTLE in focus. Built in June 1948, this engine first went to Bristol with spells at Banbury. Latterly it was allocated to Wolverhampton's Oxley shed and it was from there that it was withdrawn in February 1965. It appears to have just undergone repair and repaint – a full-scale 'sole and heel' job. No.7011 has the later type of front cover, smaller chimney and a flat-sided tender as built. I know that the drivers did not like them, but I thought they looked smashing! Note that most of the windows in the building are closed – this time, keeping the heat in!

No.3153 was one of the original Prairie tanks having been put into traffic in April 1907. Allocated to Chester prior to Nationalisation, it ended its days at Gloucester, in February 1953. The class batch ran from 3150 to 3190, all equipped with GWR Standard No.4 boilers as opposed to the Standard No.2 carried by the 51XX class. From looking at this 10th May 1953 photograph, we can see that the engine must have been stored for some time before arriving at Swindon. The smokebox is peeling, as is the paint on the side tanks, whilst the pipe is missing from the oil pot on the boiler bracket. If you look at the illustration of No.5147 on page 9, you will see that No.3153 is a later engine and had a curved front end.

58XX Nos.5805 and 5804 on shed at Swindon, 10th May 1953. Both 0-4-2Ts look ready for work as they show water from the overflow and a wisp of steam at the whistle. There is sand on the floor out of the box of No.5805 whereas the pipe is actually missing from the sandbox on 5804. Both engines were built at Swindon in January 1933 and they became Swindon allocated engines for most of their working lives. No.5804 was withdrawn in June 1959 whilst 5805 went sometime earlier in March 1958. The 58XX class were not built with auto gear for working a trailer and most did not have ATC equipment; those that did, received it rather late in life.

On 10th May 1953 this very work-stained 'Mogul' No.9303, looks as if it is in need of a major overhaul after the war. It was built here at Swindon in 1932 and had a side-window cab, screw reverser, outside steam pipes, and a short safety valve bonnet. The rear section of the frames was lengthened by 6½ inches and the 2-6-0 was renumbered as 7325 in August 1958. After that event it was transferred to Pontypool Road and was withdrawn in April 1964. Throughout its thirty-two year life it had been allocated to various sheds including Reading, Tyseley and Banbury. I saw this engine a lot in the mid-50's but now you too can see it in preservation.

Just arrived from Gloucester, '2021' class No.2121 at Swindon on 15th June 1952. Built in 1903 at Wolverhampton, the 0-6-0PT was about to be condemned.

Prairie No.3100 was one of the large versions of 2-6-2 tanks which the GWR possessed. This engine was built at Swindon in 1907 to a Churchward design and was originally numbered 3173. However, it was rebuilt by Collett in 1938 and fitted with smaller wheels, whilst the boiler was changed to one of those used by the 42XX class 2-8-0T. Four other '3150' class engines were similarly rebuilt during 1938/39, all to be used for banking duties. Others were planned to be rebuilt too but WWII put paid to that happening . Shedded at Tondu until June 1957 when it was withdrawn, No.3100 poses at Swindon on 8th August 1957. Sister No.3101 was allocated to Tyseley and used on Hatton bank – a real workhorse of an engine. I can hear it now pushing the iron ore trains up the bank – it was a fantastic sight!

'Dukedog' No.9009 was a Machynlleth engine and was withdrawn in August 1957. This 12th August 1956 photograph was taken in the Stock shed as the 4-4-0 was waiting for a decision on its future. It was built as No.3209 and carried the name EARL OF RADNOR but the names were removed in 1937. It had the frame from 'Bulldog' No.3392. These are one of my favourite locomotives and I used to see them on the Cambrian section in North Wales where we went in the early Fifties on family holidays – before my Dad found getting to Somerset was an easier trip!

33

'Castle' No.5039 RHUDDLAN CASTLE was built in 1935 and withdrawn in June 1964. It had been a Welsh engine for much of its life, variously allocated to Carmarthen and Landore with occasional short residences at Old Oak. BR Standard Cl.4 No.75047 was brand new when this picture was taken on 11th October 1953. It went to Accrington for the first two years of its life but from thereon it did not settle and worked from eight other depots before being condemned in August 1967. Many of the Standards, although liked by the footplatemen, arrived at depots as the traffic they were supposed to handle was either lost or taken over by diesels. Lots of the photographs in this book were taken on a Sunday when it would have been quiet and access would have been easy. This was a popular location to take pictures of engines ready to go back into traffic and I suppose it's a sign of the times that security was never an issue back then. So, close-up photography was the norm.

Former R.O.D. 2-8-0 No.3024 was allocated to Cardiff Canton when Keith Pirt took this photograph on 22nd August 1954. As you can see, the engine has had a quick repair – proof that BR did not believe in wasting money – a new smokebox and one piece of cladding! The ROD 2-8-0s were extremely noisy locomotives which could be heard long before you could see them at Leamington. *K.R.Pirt.*

'Castle' No.5066 SIR FELIX POLE was built in July 1937 as WARDOUR CASTLE. It was shedded at Old Oak Common and was renamed in April 1956. This is an interesting photograph taken in August 1957 when the engine had just been through the paint shop and emerged with the new BR crest, albeit of the wrong-facing variety. Two years later, in April 1959, it would be back at Swindon to be fitted with a four-row superheater (and to have the correct version of the crest applied), along with a double chimney. Then, in September 1962, it was withdrawn. What did I say about BR not wasting money!

BR Standard Cl.3 tank No.82006 was built at Swindon in May 1952 and returned there in August 1957 for a General overhaul, change of boiler and change of livery from lined black to lined passenger green. The staff at Wellington, Salop (84H), its home shed at that time, must have been pleased to get one of their 'best' locomotives [Nos.82004 and 82009 were there too!] back from Swindon looking so very posh. I think that this class was the best looking of the BR Standards. Behind the 2-6-2T was one of the classic 57XX 'Pannier' class, No.5737, a Swindon built example from 1929 with welded tanks. The 'Panniers' always looked old, even when they were modified as evidenced by the 8750 with the overhauled cab – it still looks old! Besides Swindon, outside contractors also had a hand in adding to the 0-6-0PT numbers – North British; W.G.Bagnall; Kerr, Stuart; Yorkshire Engine Co.; Beyer, Peacock; and Armstrong Whitworth – all put minor detail changes to the 'Panniers' which they supplied.

37

No.1022 COUNTY OF NORTHAMPTON was built in December 1946 and was another engine I saw all the time at Laira when it was new. The 4-6-0 transferred north to Chester in November 1951 and then in June 1958 to Shrewsbury (Salop). Like all the 'County' class engines allocated to the northern half of the region, you would see them every time you went spotting and they always seemed to be on shed at Shrewsbury if you visited on a Sunday. In this 6th May1956 photograph No.1022 is in light steam and it may be that it had just come back from a running-in turn. Look at the smokebox and you will see that it is very normal. Given the date it would be fair to suggest that the double chimney had just been fitted which would account for the fact that there is no muck in evidence. Worthy of note is that although No.1000 COUNTY OF MIDDLESEX had its own version, the double chimneys on 'County' class locomotives were unique in that they were flat-sided.

Another photograph of No.1022 COUNTY OF NORTHAMPTON. Now this is an interesting illustration, although captured some fourteen months after the previous view taken in 1956, there is evidence to suggest that it must have been into shops for a Light or Intermediate overhaul in August 1957 as it had been repainted to the later BR livery. It was withdrawn in October 1962.

Records show that Sunday 24th February 1957 was a cold dank day but for 9F No.92095 it was all bright, shiny and new as it was on its way to have its tender coupled (on the left of the photograph). It would then go off to Annesley to join numerous classmates. This was one of the locomotives that I would see going across the 'Birdcage' at Rugby on many occasions and if you weren't that lucky to share this experience, then believe me, you missed a treat! The 9Fs were put on what we called the 'Annesley Runners' which was a train of forty to fifty, unfitted, 16-ton mineral wagons full of coal. Oh Boy did they run! In fact when they hit the rails of the Great Central over-bridge at Rugby the noise was deafening. Now, that is something that wouldn't be allowed to happen today as N.I.M.B.Y's would certainly complain to Environmental Health and there would be no question as to it breaking the decibel rule! No.92095 was withdrawn in September 1966, just about the time the former GCR main line was being wound down to complete closure. *David Dalton.*

BR Standard 9F No.92208 had just been built when this photograph was taken on 6th June 1959. Eight years later, in November 1967, it was withdrawn and promptly sold for scrap! However, in the meantime, the 2-10-0 was allocated to Laira when it went into traffic on 11th June but in March 1960 it transferred to Southall, thereafter two sheds in Cardiff, followed by stints at Newton Heath and finally Kingmoor, sum up the short life of this fabulous looking machine. We have worked on two of these engines at Crewe and as with all BR Standards they have the same faults. BR knew the end was nigh when they designed the Standards and subsequently compromised on materials – little did they know that 60 years on, we would still be running them! It is fair to say however that we now have a lot of boiler work to bring them up to today's exacting standards – but I'd say it is well worth the effort. *David Dalton*.

This photograph of 'Hall' No.4916 CRUMLIN HALL and '4300' class No.7335 was taken at Swindon on Saturday 26th July 1958. The Ebbw Junction based 4-6-0 is having some last minute adjustments carried out prior to going back into traffic. The Laira based 2-6-0, on the other hand, has just acquired a new identity having been renumbered from 9313 to 7335. Although repainted, No.7335 still requires its steam pipe sleeves to be refitted but all would be in place for the twenty-six years old locomotive to go back into traffic the following week. *David Dalton.*

14XX No.1438 was built in September 1934 and went new to Reading. It was withdrawn from Oswestry in November 1962. This photograph shows that it still carried the small lion on the Welsh logo so we can assume that it had not been in the shops for some time – indeed I would, at a guess, and from the look of it, that it may well have been out of service for some time! The 0-4-2T was built as No.4338 and renumbered in October 1946. In this view you can see 0-6-0PT No.5421, which was also withdrawn from Oswestry but in October 1962. Nevertheless, they probably travelled to Swindon together. Both engines show '89D' chalked below the number. One thing is certain however, they never ran again. *David Dalton.*

'King' No.6004 – What a great shot! This is **KING GEORGE III** built in July 1927 and about to be cut up. Like so many of the 'Kings' it was withdrawn in 1962. Originally from Old Oak Common, her last shed was Cardiff Canton. This photograph from October 1962 shows her waiting with the 'Halls' and the 'Moguls'. Interestingly, they all still have their names and number plates attached. No.6004 was cut up at Swindon during the week ending Saturday 3rd November 1962. *David Dalton.*

I have included this photograph of No.7770, being cut up at Swindon, to show what a Pannier tank looked like without its tanks. You can see the asbestos around the dome which was put on like plaster and which used to be mixed in a cement mixer and applied with trowels. The cladding was then added when the 'cement' was dry. I can remember, as a boy, playing 'snowballs' with it and, on a cold day, putting cardboard in the wheelbarrow to keep it warm! No.7770 was built in February 1931 by North British Locomotive Co. It spent most of its life in South Wales and was withdrawn from Tondu shed in April 1959.

No.671 was from Alexandra (Newport & South Wales) Docks & Railway and was built as their No.16 by Hawthorn Leslie in 1889. It was withdrawn in September 1937. Take a look at that tank shape!

Swindon late 1934 – '1016' class No.1019 was built at Wolverhampton works in March 1867 and was withdrawn in September 1934. It was built with a short saddle tank and was fitted with panniers in November 1913. They were generally Northern Division engines. Visible in this photograph is the rear end of No.2658, an 'Aberdare' class 2-6-0 which was condemned in November 1934.

Posing outside the locomotive works on 24th April 1955 is outside cylinder 0-6-0PT No.1369. The little tank was built at Swindon in February 1934. Allocated to Swindon (82C) for much of the 1950s, it went to Weymouth in March 1960 and from there it was eventually withdrawn in November 1964. Interesting to note that the barrow by the side of the engine was used to carry oxygen and acetylene bottles around the works precincts!

Sister 1F PT No.1370 had a five month sojourn at Swindon in 1953 - from April to September – from its usual home at Weymouth. Here on 10th May 1953 the diminutive tank appears dwarfed by the Swindon shed coaling stage but it was supplied with an 82C shedplate for the occasion. Oh yes, the vacuum pump always looked massive on these engines.

43XX No.5390 was built in October 1920 and was re-numbered 8390 in 1944, then, in 1948, it reverted back to 5390! An Oxley engine for much of its BR life, it ended its days at Didcot and was withdrawn in August 1958. Seen here on 6th May 1956 (which must have been its last 'shopping'), the engine is fresh from the paint shop – although that doesn't apply to the tender. Such a combination was not unusual at this late date but the chances were that No.5390 was about to be coupled to a refurbished tender and the one behind was simply coupled for convenience of moving the locomotive around the works. The Mogul was fitted with outside steam pipes in 1941.

'Pannier' No.9749 was built in February 1935 and was one of the 8750 batch of 57XX with the overhauled cab. In this 6th May 1956 illustration it appears to have just been through 'shops' and is nicely presented in black livery with the 'lion and wheel' emblem although the figures on the cab side plate are not yet cleaned not make them legible. Allocated to Reading shed for much of the BR period, it was transferred to Cardiff East Dock in September 1960 but was withdrawn during the following November. If it ever went to Cardiff at all before being condemned is debatable. Nevertheless the picture is superb.

0-6-0PT No.2061 – Yes I admit to using my literary licence to illustrate my personal favourites! I really do like the Panniers – particularly the Wolverhampton built examples. This one, seen on 24th April 1955 shortly after arrival from 84H, was built in April 1899 as a saddle tank but was converted in September 1916. It had been at Stafford Road shed for years but transferred down the road to Wellington in February 1953. Its fifty-six years of loyal service were up!

'Pannier' No.7402 was built at Swindon in September 1936 and was a 74XX Class auto-fitted example with 4ft 7½in. wheels. It was withdrawn in August 1962 from Cardiff, although it had spent time at Stourbridge, Machynlleth and Carmarthen. Here in the works yard at Swindon on 13th February 1955, the 0-6-0PT looks rather resplendent after its overhaul. A point worth noting is that although these may look like the 57XX, they were a newer design built for a specific traffic.

Built for the Swansea Harbour Trust by Andrew Barclay in 1905, 0-4-0ST No.1140 was numbered 5 at the Grouping but then became GWR No.701. In 1948 it was renumbered 1140 and is seen outside the one of the shops on 25th June 1951 after a heavy overhaul. Judging from the residue on the tank side it had been through a steaming test. The cab side carries both works and number plates in a pleasing combination of information; the number plate was picked-out in red.

After a spell in 'shops', 28XX No.2877 in light steam and wearing a fresh coat of black paint, waits on the engine shed yard on 25th April 1954 prior to working back home to Canton. Built in January 1919, this 2-8-0 went new to Aberdare. It was withdrawn in February 1960. This one of course had no outside steam pipes.

The GWR acquired this former Stroudley 0-6-0T in 1940 from the bankrupt Weston, Clevedon & Portishead Railway as payment for debt. Purchased by the WC&PR from the Southern in 1925, it had formerly been LB&SCR No.43 but was renumbered and named in the Weston fleet. It remained as No.5 PORTISHEAD throughout its time on both GWR and BR(WR) until condemned and scrapped in March 1954. In this 15th June 1952 photograph, showing it stored in the Stock shed, it still carries the GWR logo on the side tank leaving nobody in doubt as to who owned the 1877 vintage engine. A sister engine, WC&PR No.6, another ex-Brighton product of even older vintage, was also acquired by the GWR in 1940.

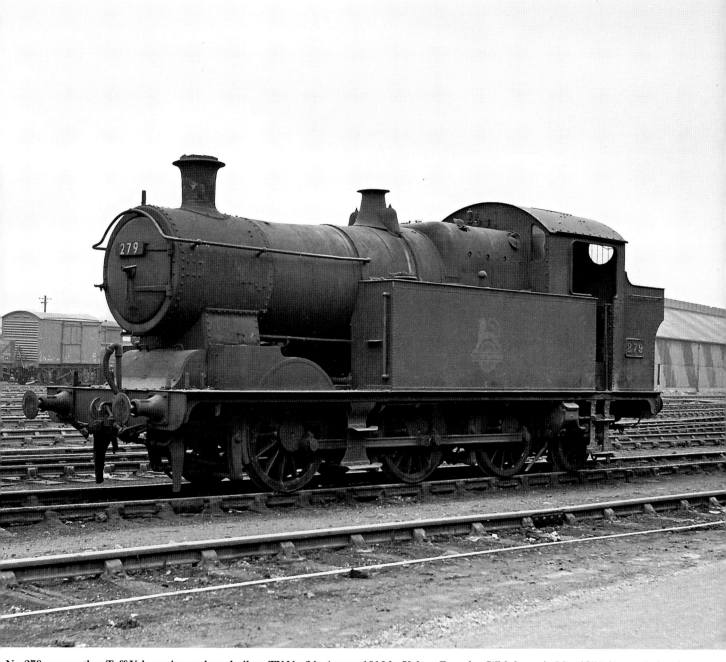

No.279 was another Taff Vale engine and was built as TV No.2 in August 1910 by Vulcan Foundry. Withdrawn in May 1954, it was obviously putting in some time as a works shunter as this 13th February 1955 photograph suggests. Latterly it had been allocated to the sheds at Treherbert, Abercynon and Cardiff East Dock. Note the further use of wartime camouflage on the building across the tracks.

BR Standard 8P No.71000 DUKE OF GLOUCESTER, complete with Crewe North shed plate, stands outside the works on 31st October 1954 with 9F No.92001 for company. The Pacific had come to Swindon for tests, which proved nothing and found nothing untoward! Although BR was supposed to be one organisation, and had been formed for nearly seven years when 71000 went for testing, the somewhat uncooperative and anti anything not GWR brigade, were alive and well and living and working in Swindon. The 9F design had a similar reception on the WR when it arrived. No.71000 is still with us today and represents the first 'miracle' of preservation (in more ways than one), as its original cylinders were removed with one set going to the Science museum whilst the other was kept back at Crewe.

BR Standard Cl.3 No.82007 is seen here on 15th June 1952, as brand new and just out of the shops. It would soon be on its way to Tyseley, the first of a dozen different sheds it would call home – including all three Bristol depots - over the next twelve years before withdrawal. It is in steam and is an example to all modellers who don't like to weather engines, that even though it has yet to be allocated, it is already dirty.

Mogul No.6387 was built in August 1921 and went to Carmarthen. For the five years from 1950 it was allocated to Swindon after which it went to Banbury. It was withdrawn from Worcester in June 1962. In this 30th August 1953 photograph it is out of steam and stored with a classmate, a 'Dukedog' bringing up the rear. If you look closely at the two tenders you will see that they are different with No.6387 having a larger 4000 gallon intermediate type. In the background can be seen the Swindon gas works, which was still in camouflage.

25th April 1954 and newly delivered 0-6-0PT No.8444 becomes the latest member of the 94XX class of Pannier tanks. Built by Bagnall & Co, (note the side tank), this class was not only built at Swindon and Stafford but also by Robert Stephenson & Co., and Yorkshire Engine Co. They were not popular with their crews and No.8444, which went to Aberdare was withdrawn in August 1963. Interesting to me are the boilers lined up in the background, including one that would have been a Pannier boiler which had freshly made asbestos cement applied. Of further interest is the WD tender on the right; this has a chalked inscription 5-324 (its BR designation which would be plated on the rear end during this visit to works) on its side sheet and was the tender formerly attached to WD No.90323 which had visited Swindon earlier in the year to change tenders.

Yet another Pannier! This is No.2716 in September 1950. In mitigation, these engines were as rare as hen's teeth by 1950 so I think I am
allowed to include it! Built at Wolverhampton in November 1896 as a saddle tank, it was a member of Class 655. That particular class
represented the last of the large tanks to be built at Wolverhampton. Panniers were fitted in March 1924. No.2716 was withdrawn from
Croes Newydd in September 1950, outlasted by No.1782 which succumbed eight weeks later. On the right of the photograph was '850'
class Pannier No.1989, another Wolverhampton built tank which was condemned in October, and was ex Gloucester shed. Note how small
the '850s' were.

Photographed at Swindon in November 1950, No.46 was from yet another Welsh concern – the Rhymney Railway – and it was their No.97.
Built in December 1909 by Robert Stephenson, it was withdrawn in August 1950 after being repainted in black with the full BRITISH
RAILWAYS logo on the side tanks. Unfortunately we can only speculate as to why this was carried out since it was withdrawn from Radyr.
Worthy of note is the sliding cab side sheets for the blackout.

Although undated, this photograph shows 2-4-0 Crane Engine No.1299 at some time between the wars. From the South Devon Railway, it was converted to a crane in 1881. A useful piece of kit to have around a place like Swindon, It was finally condemned and withdrawn in 1936. To the right is another crane engine – one of three to be built from Pannier tanks at Swindon during 1901. They were both numbered and named as follows: 16 HERCULES allocated to Swindon, 17 CYCLOPS allocated to Wolverhampton, and 18 STEROPES also at Swindon. All three were withdrawn in 1936.

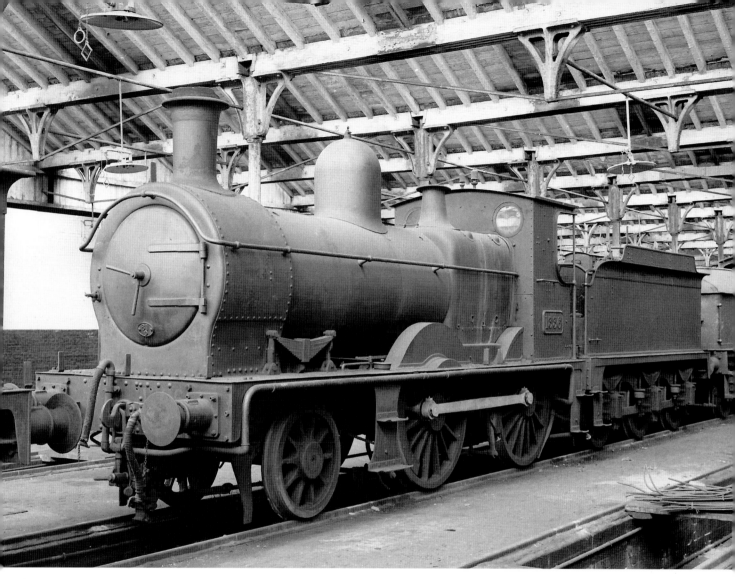

1P 2-4-0 No.1336 was the last of its compatriots still in service when this photograph was taken inside the Stock shed on 14th September 1952. The other two former M&SWJ 2-4-0s, Nos.1334 and 1335, had been condemned that very month. No.1336 started life as M&SWJ No.12 and was built by Dubs & Co. in 1894. Allocated to Reading, and obviously kept serviceable for a purpose, this engine was not withdrawn until March 1954.

Unfortunately this undated photograph of the former Powlesland & Mason 0-4-0ST No.1153 gives us few clues as to why the saddletank was sat on the works reception lines at Swindon. Note that the coupling and connecting rods are detached, as was usual when these diminutive four-coupled tanks had to travel any distance – Swansea to Swindon was quite a distance for these little chaps. Up to May 1953 No.1153 was allocated to Danygraig but was then transferred to Reading. In January 1954 it was returned to Danygraig but was immediately transferred to the former LNWR shed at Swansea Victoria from where it worked until withdrawn in October 1955. Now, in this illustration was the engine arriving at Swindon for overhaul, or even withdrawal? Was it en route to or returning from Reading? Besides the rods being absent, a piece of what we can only presume to be timber has been placed onto the bottom slide bar; no doubt to prevent the piston being drawn into the cylinder by vacuum or whatever during the journey.

I just had to include this photograph from 27th August 1956. Newly built at Swindon, this is one of the cross-country diesel multiple units and as such shows up the problems of BR in the 1950s and its push for modernisation. Although I find it quite attractive - probably because it is quite bizarre – it is basically a Mark 1 coach with a rather unflattering cab added. If you look at the buffer beam, even this, in itself, is weird. What this photograph highlights is that there were problems manufacturing modern equipment with designers and engineers who were used to steam age technology. They were simply over-engineered, complicated and costly to run and maintain. Ironically, some thirty years later, in its quest for speed and further modernisation, BR introduced aviation technology when designing the Advanced Passenger Train (APT) but that particular type of engineering was not up to the rigours of the railway industry and it too was a failure.

18000 was built by Brown-Boveri in Switzerland in 1946 but it was not put into BR stock until June 1950. Its weight restricted the sphere of operation and it could only run on the same routes as the 'King' class. The wheel arrangement was A-1-A+A-1-A – same as the later 'Westerns' note – but it was not a success and spent a lot of time at Swindon works where, on more than one occasion, it caught fire. Eventually it was sold back to Brown-Boveri and returned to Switzerland where it was used to trial new ideas but with the gas-turbine removed. It was brought back to the UK for the opening of the new Freightliner terminal at Willesden and was then sold to my Trust. It is a big engine and although it will never run again, at least we are still able to look at it. *I.W.Coulson, 5th May 1960.*

Gas-turbine 18000, shown here at the end of its working life; the locomotive is in green livery and is looking the worse for wear. In this May 1960 illustration you can see from the state of the side frames that the fuel spewed everywhere. It was not a pleasant drive either, as the crew always smelt of fuel oil! *C.J.B.Sandersson.*

Another interesting picture, this one depicts 18000 in green livery but with the early British Railways emblem. It is also carrying a Train Register board.

18000 as built. The gas-turbine had not long been in service when this picture was taken. The livery is black with silver and what is interesting is the fact that it was taken in the same position as the previous picture, outside 'A' shop.

18100 was ordered by the Great Western in the mid-40's but, due to the war, and then changes made by BTC, it was not delivered to Swindon until December 1951. It was built in Manchester by the Metropolitan-Vickers company. 18100 was also a gas-turbine but unlike 18000 it was run on aviation kerosene whereas the 18000 was built to run on heavy fuel oil. The 18100 was more successful in traffic than 18000, but it was 'in the wrong place at the wrong time' and even the controls had to be simplified. This undated photograph shows 18100 at Swindon where it was stored for some years before being sent to Bowsfield works in Stockton-on-Tees where it was rebuilt into a pure electric locomotive to run from overhead collection at 25kV as E1000 (E2001). It was then used for testing on the Manchester-Crewe section of the newly energized West Coast electrification. It ended its days at Rugby where I saw it whilst working for the General Electric Company.